Decade of terrorism

Such issues mattered, because terrorism became a worldwide problem in the 1970s. The Palestinians, in their struggle against Israel, targeted individuals and countries they regarded as their enemy's supporters. Conflict in Northern Ireland spread to mainland Britain when the IRA (Irish Republican Army) started a bombing campaign there. Other violent groups included the Angry Brigade (Britain), the Baader-Meinhof gang (West Germany), the Red Brigades (Italy), the Weathermen (USA), the Japanese Red Army and the Tupumaros (Uruguay).

Ongoing struggle

The 1972 killing of Israeli athletes at the Munich Olympics, and the kidnapping and murder of the Italian statesman Aldo Moro (1978), were among the many terrorist outrages of the 1970s. Terrorism became international as groups with different aims sometimes worked together. For example, in 1975 the notorious revolutionary 'Carlos the Jackal' (Illich Ramirez Sanchez) helped the Palestinians by taking the ministers of the Arab oil states as hostages. However, the terrorists also suffered defeats. The Baader-Meinhof gang were captured in 1972, and in 1976 the Israelis staged a daring attack on a hijacked plane at Entebbe in Uganda, rescuing the hostages and killing the hijackers. But by the end of the 1970s the struggle against terrorism was far from won.

Aldo Moro, a former Italian prime minister, is shown in a photo taken by the Red Brigades terrorists, who kidnapped him in 1978. Moro appears with the Red Brigades' flag in the background. The Italian government refused to accept the terrorists' demands, and Moro was murdered.

eye witness

At two-thirty in the morning, I was awakened.... They wanted me up front, for questioning.... I went and was told to sign a piece of paper ... but I couldn't sign because my hand was shaking. They told us to get off the plane ... not knowing where I was going, not knowing when I would see my family again ... I was sure I was going to be killed.... We were put on board a bus. It was myself and nine other people.... Two guerrillas sat up front carrying machine guns facing us – as if we were going to run somewhere.

David Raab (a 17-year-old hostage in 1970),
Terror in Black September (Palgrave Macmillan, 2007)

- **SEE ALSO**
  Pages 10–11: 5 September 1972
  Murder at the Munich Olympics
  Pages 14–15: 6 October 1973
  Egypt and Syria Attack Israel

- **FURTHER INFORMATION**
  Books:
  Terrorism and Security
  by Nick Hunter (Raintree, 2012)
  Websites:
  www.bbc.co.uk/history/recent/sept_11/
  changing_faces_01.shtml
  A handy seven-page BBC history and discussion of terrorism

16 DECEMBER 1971

Bangladesh is Born

On 16 December 1971, India emerged victorious from a two-week conflict with Pakistan. In the eastern sector of the war, the Pakistani commander, General Niazi, and his entire army surrendered unconditionally. The ceremony was held in public at Dhaka, the capital of what had been East Pakistan (also known as East Bengal). India's victory ensured that East Pakistan's struggle for independence succeeded, and the former province became the new nation of Bangladesh.

Two Pakistans

Britain had ruled the Indian sub-continent until 1947, when it was divided into two newly independent states, India and Pakistan. Pakistan consisted of two geographically distinct regions. West Pakistan and East Pakistan were separated by 1,600 kilometres of Indian territory, and the Bengali-speaking people in the eastern province were different in character and traditions from those in the west. The centres of government and power were located in West Pakistan, so the east, despite its larger population, was neglected. Resentment built up until December 1970, when elections were held throughout Pakistan. All the East Pakistan seats were won by the Awami League, which demanded autonomy (self-rule) for the province.

Three children from a Bangladeshi border village, newly arrived at a refugee camp. Huge numbers of people fled to India when the Pakistan army brutally suppressed the independence movement.

What the papers said

It was a day of many dramatic happenings. First there was no response until the eleventh hour from the Pakistan military command in the East to the call for surrender.... Finally came the surrender to Lieutenant-General J S Aurora, commander of the Indian forces and the Mukti Bahini (the Bangla Desh fighters) in the East, who flew by helicopter to Dacca.... Mrs Gandhi, the Indian Prime Minister, who broke the news to Parliament ... was given a hero's ovation such as has never been seen in the two Houses before.

Kulddip Nayar, The Times, 16 December 1971

6

Contents

GLOBAL EVENTS

BRITISH EVENTS

Three Hijacked Airliners are Blown Up

The explosions were set off in Dawson's Field, a disused airstrip in the Jordanian Desert. The planes belonged to British, American and Swiss airlines. They had been hijacked by Palestinian terrorists, who destroyed them when they believed a rescue attempt was starting. They removed the passengers and released most of them. But the fleeing terrorists took more than 50 passengers with them and held them as hostages. It seemed likely that they would be killed unless the Palestinians' demands were met.

The first of the three hijacked airliners explodes at Dawson's Field in the Jordanian Desert. After the destruction of the other two, the terrorists left the scene with their hostages.

Deal or No Deal?

Some governments decided to do a deal. Britain, West Germany and Switzerland released several imprisoned terrorists, and in return the hostages from their countries were freed. On one level the deal was a success. But it highlighted the difficult issue of how governments should respond to hijackings and hostage-taking. If they gave way to the terrorists' demands, the terrorists won and would be encouraged to carry on. Refusing to negotiate would foil and eventually discourage them.

However, such a tough attitude risked the lives of innocent hostages, and few governments felt able to act entirely consistently.

Scene of triumph: smiling Indian Brigadier General Misra leads his troops into Dhaka, the capital of East Pakistan. After the fall of the city, Pakistan was forced to agree to a ceasefire, and the war ended in India's favour. As a result, East Pakistan became an independent country under its new name, Bangladesh.

A revolt crushed

The Pakistan government was reluctant to accept the result, and people in East Pakistan began to talk of independence. But the government struck first. In March 1971, martial law was imposed and the Awami leader, Sheikh Mujibur Rahman, was arrested – but not before he made a radio broadcast proclaiming an independent East Pakistan, now renamed Bangladesh. Bengali units of the Pakistan army rallied to the new state, but troops from the west were airlifted in and crushed the revolt. The savage behaviour of the Pakistani forces led to thousands of deaths, and millions of Bangladeshis fled to neighbouring India.

War and independence

Relations between India and Pakistan had often been strained, and they grew worse when India began to help Bangladeshi guerrillas. In December, war broke out between India and Pakistan. Fierce struggles in the west ended in stalemate. But, unexpectedly, the Indian army advanced rapidly in the east with the help of Bangladeshi guerrillas, and won a swift victory. Bangladesh had won its independence, and Sheikh Mujibur Rahman became its first prime minister. However, the new country found it hard to achieve stability, and a long period of violence and uncertainty followed a coup that overthrew Rahman in 1975.

- **SEE ALSO**
  Pages 24–25: 29 April 1975
  Saigon Falls to the North Vietnamese
  Pages 36–37: 1 February 1979
  Ayatollah Khomeini Returns to Iran

- **FURTHER INFORMATION**
  Books:
  It's Cool to Learn About Countries: Bangladesh
  by Tamara Orr
  (Cherry Lake Publishing, 2010)
  Websites:
  www.bbc.co.uk/news/world-south-asia-12650940
  Bangladesh overview, key facts and leaders

President Nixon Visits China

At 11.30 a.m. the American president's official plane, Air Force One, reached the airport at Beijing, the capital of China. President Richard Nixon walked down the gangway to the runway, where the Chinese prime minister, Chou En Lai, was waiting to greet him. The two men shook hands. It was a significant moment. Their countries had been bitter enemies for over twenty years, but that was about to change.

A famous meeting

When the official ceremonies were over, the president and his party were driven in a motorcade through Beijing. The Chinese had arranged a week-long programme of conferences, banquets and tourist activities for their guests. But the Americans were worried because they had not been given a definite promise that Nixon would meet China's ruler, Mao Zedong. Fortunately Mao, though old and in poor health, was eager to see Nixon, and asked the president to visit his house in the afternoon. There followed another handshake – photographed and published world-wide – and an hour of friendly private conversations between the leaders and their advisers. Mao even pretended jokingly that he had voted for Nixon.

Enemy powers

US-Chinese enmity dated from 1949, when the communists, led by Mao, won the civil war against the Nationalists, who had been supported by the United States. The USA refused to recognize the new communist republic, and protected the defeated Nationalists, who had retreated to the island of Taiwan. War in Korea (1950-53) and other events in Asia reinforced US-Chinese hostility.

Easing conflicts

In 1949 China had allied itself with its fellow-communist regime, the Soviet Union. But by the 1960s the two powers had become enemies. Isolated, China was ravaged by internal upheavals, notably Mao's disastrous 'Cultural Revolution'. When China began to

⦿ eye witness

Most memorable were my meetings with Chou and Mao. We learned later that Mao had already suffered a mild stroke, although the Chinese people did not know it. He was still treated with enormous respect by his aides and attendants and was sharp in his repartee.... His office was cluttered with books – not for show, but for reading ... he said he had read *Six Crises* [a book by Nixon] and found that 'it was not a bad book'. Also ... he showed his political acumen when he said, 'I voted for you during your last election.'

Richard Nixon, *In the Arena* (Simon and Schuster, 1990)

The famous handshake: Nixon meets Chairman Mao in Beijing during his historic visit to China in February 1972.

emerge from isolation, Nixon recognized that the international situation was changing. He showed considerable courage in contacting the Chinese unofficially and then accepting an invitation to their country. The meeting with Mao was important because it convinced most Americans that the trip had been a success. The United States and China did not become allies, but conflict was now less likely. Simultaneously, the USA improved its relations with the Soviet Union, making treaties to limit the nuclear arms race between them. This began a period of détente (easing of international tensions) which lasted until the end of the 1970s.

• **SEE ALSO**
Pages 20–21: 8 August 1974
Nixon Announces his Resignation

• **FURTHER INFORMATION**

Books:
China by Patrick Catel
(Heinemann Library, 2012)

Websites:
http://news.bbc.co.uk/onthisday/hi/dates/stories/february/21/newsid_2728000/2728761.stm
Nixon's visit to China

Murder at the Munich Olympics

The 1972 Olympic Games were held at Munich in southern Germany. As usual, competitors were housed in their own Olympic Village, and because of terrorist threats the Village was heavily policed. But on the night of 5 September, towards the end of the Games, five men, dressed like athletes in track suits, managed to climb into the Israeli compound. They made contact with three others who had bluffed their way in with false documents. The men all belonged to Black September, a Palestinian terrorist group.

A Black September terrorist stands defiantly on the balcony of the Israeli team's quarters in the Olympic village. The terrorists have seized hostages and are making their demands known.

Armed with sub-machine guns, the terrorists attacked the building that housed the Israelis. A wrestling coach was shot down and a weight-lifter died helping fellow sportsmen to escape. The terrorists captured nine Israeli athletes and held them as hostages, threatening to kill them if security forces attacked. The terrorists stated their demands: the release of hundreds of jailed Palestinians and other prisoners, including two convicted German terrorists. The West German government appeared to give way. The gang and its hostages were taken by helicopter to an airport to be flown to Egypt.

Failed rescue

In reality, the West Germans had prepared a trap. As the terrorists and their hostages crossed the tarmac to board the waiting plane, the airport lights were turned out. Police sharpshooters were in position and ready to pick off the Palestinians. But they failed to kill them all and there was a gun battle. At its end, four of the terrorists had been killed and three had been captured; only one managed to escape. All nine of the Israeli hostages were dead. Black September had not won, but the rescue attempt had failed disastrously.

Palestinians and Israelis

The attack on the Israeli compound was a shocking episode in a long and painful conflict. The founding of the Jewish state of Israel in 1948, and Israel's victories over Arab states, left millions of Palestinians as refugees or living under Israeli occupation. The Palestinians founded guerrilla and terrorist organizations, most of them grouped together as the PLO (Palestine Liberation Organization), to attack Israel. By also committing terrorist acts in other countries, the Palestinians hoped to publicize their plight while hurting Israel and its supporters. The policy brought some successes, but in the long run generated anger rather than sympathy. Finally, in 1988, the PLO publicly gave up terrorism, though progress on the Palestinian-Israeli issue remained limited.

During the funeral service in Tel Aviv, Israel, a woman weeps beside the coffin of one of the 11 Israeli athletes.

What the papers said

As they [the terrorists] tried to rush the Israelis, they were halted at the door by a coach.... Tuvia Sokolsky ... said ... 'I heard this shout: "Boys, get out!" I saw a strange picture – one of the men on the team ... using all his strength to keep the door closed.... I think he saved my life. Because of the warning, I was able to escape from the room.' Gus Psabari, a wrestler, dashed out in a hail of bullets.... 'I think I ran faster than [Olympic sprinter] Valery Borzov; I think I broke the record for the dash.'

David Binder in the *New York Times*, 6 September 1972

- **SEE ALSO**
  Pages 4–5: 12 September 1970
  Three Hijacked Airliners are Blown Up

- **FURTHER INFORMATION**
  📖 Books:
  Terror at the Munich Olympics
  by Courtney Farrell
  (Abdo Publishing Company, 2010)
  Websites:
  www.time.com/time/archive/collections.
  0,21428,c_munich,00.shtml
  Time magazine articles from the Munich
  Olympics

Chile's Government is Overthrown

Trouble started at 6 a.m., when Chilean naval units occupied the port of Valparaiso. The defence minister, Orlando Letellier, informed the president, Salvador Allende. Then Letellier went to his ministry in the Chilean capital, Santiago. Military men were waiting for him, and he was immediately arrested. A radio broadcast announced the formation of a new government, drawn from the chiefs of the armed forces. But Allende refused to resign and leave the country. At about 9 a.m. he made a broadcast on the only radio station not in rebel hands. Though defiant, he made it clear that he was expecting to die.

The palace besieged

Soon afterwards, military units and Sherman tanks surrounded the presidential palace and bombarded it. Loyal guards and policemen fought back with bazookas and machine guns, although the enemy's superior numbers were bound to triumph. After a brief truce, during which the women in the palace were allowed to leave, jets struck with rockets and bombs. The two-hour siege ended when soldiers stormed the blazing building. Allende was found dead, having apparently killed himself rather than be captured. The new military regime, headed by General Augusto Pinochet, dealt savagely with Allende's supporters. A 17-year dictatorship followed, creating deep divisions between Chileans that continued into the 21st century.

The La Moneda presidential palace under siege. Rebel Chilean troops fire down on the palace from a rooftop during the coup that overthrew Chile's elected president, Salvador Allende, on 11 September 1973. Allende himself died in the attack.

Latin America

Allende died because his government's policies threatened powerful interests. His Socialist Party was pledged to nationalize (transfer from private to government control) important interests and improve the lives of the poor. The government's enemies included the rich and powerful, and also the United States, whose Central Intelligence Agency (CIA) was involved in planning and funding the coup. Allende's overthrow was striking because his government had been democratically elected in 1970 and again in 1973.

In Chile, as in most of Latin America, political stability was hard to achieve. The gulf between rich and poor was very wide, and reforms that might lessen the power and privileges of the rich were fiercely resisted. The dominant regional power, the United States, was determined to defend American business interests in the region. The USA was also suspicious of radical and socialist movements, fearing that if they gained power they would become allies of the Soviet Union, as Cuba had done. US interventions in Latin American countries continued into the 21st century.

General Augusto Pinochet (left) with Chilean president Salvador Allende. In August 1973, Allende appointed Pinochet head of the armed forces. Three weeks later Pinochet launched the coup that overthrew him.

⊙ eye witness

The following eye witness account of the scene in Santiago reached Buenos Aires after the reporter, Agustin Giannoni, had been held for hours at gunpoint by rebel soldiers: 'We have now spent 14 hours in our semi-destroyed office in ... Santiago – windows broken, no telephone, no water, no food. In the neighbouring office ... women – two of them wounded – crying and screaming hysterically. Others weep silently. The streets are empty except for military patrols. The predominant sound is machine-gun fire. The only news we have tells of hundreds dead, but the most recent report speaks of 4,500.... Everyone now is scared stiff.'

The Guardian, 14 September 1973

- • **SEE ALSO**
  Pages 24–25: 29 April 1975
  Saigon Falls to the North Vietnamese
  Pages 38–39: 24 December 1979
  Soviet Forces Enter Afghanistan

- • **FURTHER INFORMATION**
  📖 Books:
  Chile by Marion Morrison (Raintree, 2012)
  Websites:
  http://h2g2.com/approved_entry/A716591
  The 1973 coup in Chile

Egypt and Syria Attack Israel

Early in the afternoon, Syrian planes attacked Israeli positions on the Golan Heights, Syrian territory held by Israel since 1967. A few minutes later, 400 kilometres to the west, Egyptian commandos launched an assault across the Suez Canal against Israel's fortified Bar-Lev line on the east bank. 6 October was a day when Jews fasted and did not travel – Yom Kippur, which gave its name to the war that followed.

Yom Kippur War

The co-ordinated Syrian-Egyptian offensives took the Israelis by surprise. The Golan and Suez were only lightly defended, since most of Israel's army were reservists – trained men and women who led ordinary civilian lives unless they were called up during a war. During the first few days of the Yom Kippur War, Israel was in peril while it struggled to mobilize its forces. Syrian tanks drove the Israelis back across the Golan Heights. The Egyptians broke through the Bar-Lev line, and Israel's air force suffered heavy casualties in its attempts to stem their advance.

Holding on

For two days it was unclear who had the upper hand. In the most vulnerable sector, the Golan, Israeli tanks just held on until reinforcements arrived and the Syrians were forced to retreat.

War on the Golan Heights: Israeli artillery pounds the Syrian positions. The Israeli soldiers are covering their ears to protect themselves from the deafening noise.

The main Israeli effort was then directed against the Egyptians. On 15 October, in a daring move, Israeli units landed on the west bank of the Suez Canal and cut off the Egyptian army in Sinai. By the 26th, when a United Nations ceasefire came into force, the Egyptian Third Army was encircled and Israeli tanks were within 65 kilometres of the Syrian capital, Damascus.

Road to peace

Israel had won, though at a heavy cost. However, the war had an even greater impact on Egypt, which had fought well enough to banish the memory of earlier defeats. This may have made it easier for Egypt's president, Anwar Sadat, to follow a bold new policy. He ended Egypt's close relationship with the Soviet Union and sought aid and friendship from the United States. Even more boldly, he began talks with Israel that culminated in the 1979 Camp David agreement. Under its terms, Egypt recovered the vast area of Sinai it had lost in the 1967 war, and made peace with Israel. This seemed like a major breakthrough. However, there was no peace between Israel and other Arab states. The Middle East remained a dangerously tense region.

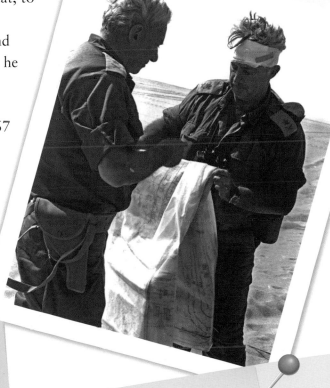

Discussion in the desert: Israeli generals Ariel Sharon (right) and Haim Bar-Lev consult the map, shortly after the Israeli landings on the west bank of the Suez Canal that turned the Yom Kippur War against Egypt.

◉ eye witness

That Yom Kippur morning ... three Phantoms flying north ... evoked some astonishment. Those planes were just about the only machines in motion ... anywhere in Israel.... At 2 in the afternoon ... I noticed to my amazement clusters of people huddled round transistor radios as well as a sudden movement of traffic.... Taxis were handing out mobilization orders. I saw several men receive them on the street ... they went back into their homes, reappearing ... in their army uniforms and carrying their guns. With a hasty farewell to their families, they were on their way to ... their units at the front.

Theodore Friedman, quoted in L Soshak and A L Eisenberg, *Momentous Century* (Cornwall books, 1984)

- **SEE ALSO**
  Pages 4–5: 12 September 1970
  Three Hijacked Airlines are Blown Up

- **FURTHER INFORMATION**
  📖 Books:
  The Arab-Israeli War Since 1948
  by Alex Woolf (Heinemann, 2012)
  Websites:
  www.bbc.co.uk/learningzone/clips/the-yom-kippur-war/10213.html
  Video and background about the Yom Kippur War

The Price of Oil Soars

Sheikh Ahmed Zaki Yamani made a statement on 17 October that had worldwide consequences. Yamani was the head of OPEC, an organization that brought together the world's major oil-exporting countries. OPEC was dominated by Saudi Arabia and other Arab states, although it also included non-Arab countries such as Iran, Nigeria and Venezuela. Yamani announced the previous day's decision – to raise the price of OPEC's oil dramatically, from US$3.00 to US$5.12 a barrel.

eye witness

Two very separate issues were at stake. One had political implications. That was the war and the question of oil as a political instrument.... The other was the price of oil.... I realized the political and economic impact of the date [of the OPEC decision] as soon as it happened.... For the first time the producers faced the consumers of the industrialized countries without anyone in the middle. October 16 was the demarcation. It was the day that OPEC seized power. Real power.

Sheikh Yamani, quoted in Jeffrey Robinson, *Yamani: The Inside Story* (Simon & Schuster, 1988)

The oil-rich states would now earn much more money. But the Arab producers also had a political motive, prompted by the Yom Kippur War. To punish states that they saw as supporters of Israel, oil production was to be reduced, and an embargo cut off supplies to the United States and the Netherlands. New cutbacks and price increases were introduced before the end of 1973, when crude (unprocessed) oil sold at almost four times the price it had been a few years earlier.

Panic reactions

Oil was vital to the running of advanced economies such as those of North America, Western Europe and Japan. Supplied via Western-based oil companies, these economies had enjoyed

Sheikh Ahmed Zaki Yamani, Saudi Arabia's Oil Minister, speaks at a press conference in London during talks on the 1973 oil crisis.

In Britain, as in other countries, the oil crisis caused panic buying of petrol. Long queues at garages like this one were a common sight.

decades of cheap fuel. Now, for the first time, the oil producers were not negotiating but naming their price. The increases caused genuine shortages and also panic reactions. Vehicles formed long queues at the petrol pumps, despite soaring prices. In the United States, speed limits were imposed to reduce consumption. The high price of oil increased some countries' dependence on other fuels. In Britain, after British coal miners went on strike, the fuel shortage was so severe that a three-day working week was introduced in January 1974.

Long-term effects

In time, the advanced economies adjusted to higher fuel prices. The embargo against the Netherlands and the United States ended in November 1973 and March 1974 respectively. The Arabs' use of oil as a political weapon had only limited success, exerting some influence on Western European and Japanese attitudes. However, the crisis had serious long-term effects. A worldwide depression was avoided. But in many countries, inflation (rising general price levels) and unemployment became a problem, and it became harder to export enough goods to pay for expensive fuel imports. Vast wealth flowed into the oil states. Elsewhere, governments encouraged a search for alternative energy sources, such as North Sea oil and gas. For the first time, energy had become a major concern of political policy.

- **SEE ALSO**
  Pages 14–15: 6 October 1973
  Egypt and Syria Attack Israel

- **FURTHER INFORMATION**
  Books:
  The Arabian Peninsula in the Age of Oil
  by John Calvert (Mason Crest Publishers, 2007)
  Websites:
  www.opec.org/opec_web/en/about_us/24.htm
  A brief history of OPEC

Sydney Opera House Opens

It was a great moment for Australians. Masses of balloons were released. Australian air force planes flew overhead. People around Sydney Harbour cheered, and hundreds of boats sounded their horns. Queen Elizabeth II, as sovereign of Australia, had just declared Sydney Opera House open. Later in the day, Beethoven's Ninth Symphony became the first work performed in the building.

A controversial project

The opening marked the triumphant end to a long-running and controversial project. It began in 1956 with a competition for the best design for a proposed new opera house. The site chosen was spectacular – Bennelong Point, a narrow strip of land thrusting into the harbour. The winner of the competition was an almost unknown young Danish architect, Jørn Utzon, whose design broke with the dominant box-like 'modernist' style of architecture. Instead, the opera house was to cover the entire point and to culminate in a series of shell roofs. From some angles it looked like a boat with huge sails, about to launch into the harbour. However, work on the opera house was painfully slow. Years passed and costs soared. Arguments flared, and Utzon resigned from the project in 1966. But when the building was completed, Australians were proud of it and its image became a symbol of Sydney and Australia.

Sydney Opera House, with its multiple shell roofs and spectacular harbour setting, is recognized as one of the great 20th-century buildings.

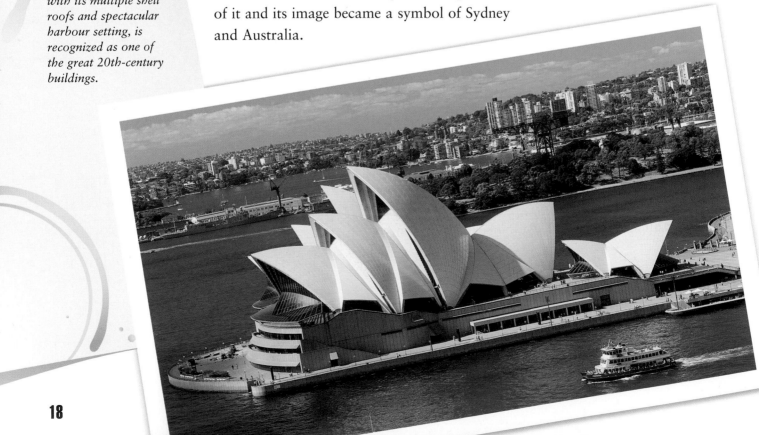

The Twin Towers

Other striking buildings were completed in the 1970s. New York's World Trade Center, the 'Twin Towers', was designed by the American architect Minoru Yamasaki with brilliant light-reflecting aluminium sheathing on the outside. The Center was not a single building, but consisted of two identical 110-storey towers, at the time the tallest structures on earth. Their position on the skyline made them a symbol of New York until they were tragically destroyed by terrorists in 2001.

The Beaubourg

The Pompidou Centre, or Beaubourg, in Paris was designed by British architect Richard Rogers and his Italian partner Renzo Piano. It was a centre for the arts with a large open piazza (forecourt) where people could relax or perform. The outside was lined with features normally hidden inside – huge pipes, funnels and fuse boxes supplying the water, electricity and air conditioning, all painted in bright colours. Also on the outside, a transparent-sided escalator zigzagged to the top floor. At first regarded as bizarre, designs of this kind were to become increasingly common in modern architecture.

The Pompidou Centre, Paris. The outside, with pipes and other brightly coloured service features, was new and startling in the 1970s.

What the papers said

This was the grand leap of the imagination that Australia badly needed but had not yet made. Some older and more conservative local architects objected to the design as fanciful. And in between, through a barrage of publicity and cross-argument such as no building had ever received from the Australian press ... it became ... a cult object of enthusiasm, dissent, jokes and hobnailed political infighting.... Still, there it is, ... ready now for its ceremonial visit by Queen Elizabeth II – an Opera House that marks a watershed in Australian cultural history.

Australian art critic Robert Hughes in Time, 8 October 1973

• **FURTHER INFORMATION**
📖 Books:
Sydney Opera House
by Sheelagh Matthews (Weigl Publishers, 2008)
💾 Websites:
http://www.sydneyoperahouse.com/about/
house_history_landing.aspx
A history of the Sydney Opera House

08

Nixon Announces his Resignation

At 9 p.m., 61-year-old President Richard M Nixon spoke to the American people on television and radio. He told them that he intended to resign at noon the following day. Nixon became the first and only American president to resign his office. He claimed that he was going because he no longer had enough support in Congress (the body that makes US laws) to govern effectively. But most observers believed the real reason was Nixon's fear of impeachment – of being put on trial in Congress for trying to cover up the long-running Watergate scandal.

Illegal activities

Nixon's up-and-down political career peaked when he was finally elected president in 1968 and enjoyed some striking successes. He ended the long and painful US involvement in Vietnam and greatly improved relations with communist China and the Soviet Union. In November 1972 Nixon won a landslide victory and a second four-year term as president. However, the event that would ruin him had already taken place.

Richard Nixon tells the nation that he intends to resign as US president. He enjoyed considerable success until he was brought down by the Watergate scandal.

What the papers said

A President of the United States has resigned from office. It is a profoundly sad and profoundly heartening occasion. The sadness all but speaks for itself. Richard Nixon, a man whose entire adult professional life was dedicated to the quest for and exercise of the powers of the office of the presidency, leaves that office under a cloud of wrongdoing and shame.... [It is heartening because] it required the courage and ultimate decency and good sense of many ... in public life to reaffirm those standards of public conduct against which he was judged and found wanting.

Washington Post, 9 August 1974

Bob Woodward (left) and Carl Bernstein, writers for the Washington Post *newspaper. Their investigations and reporting did much to expose the Watergate scandal.*

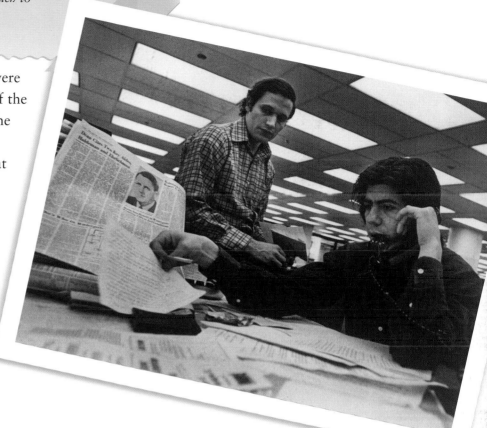

On 17 June 1972, five burglars were caught trying to bug the offices of the opposition Democratic Party in the Watergate building, Washington, DC. It gradually became clear that 'Watergate' had been part of an illegal campaign to spy on and discredit people opposed to Nixon's re-election. More and more links emerged between the burglars and the president's residence, the White House. In April 1973, top presidential advisers and government members were forced to resign and later went to prison.

Tell-tale tapes

Nixon protested that he had not known about the illegalities. But he refused to hand over tapes on which his conversations and phone calls were recorded. And when the special prosecutor Archibald Cox demanded the tapes, Nixon dismissed him. The president wielded great power, but journalists, Congressmen and lawyers doggedly sought to discover the truth. When the US Supreme Court forced Nixon to hand over the tapes, they showed that he knew a good deal about attempts to cover up the crime. The taped conversations also showed an ugly side to Nixon, including an almost insane hatred of journalists and 'enemies', which helped to turn public feeling against him. After the first steps were taken towards impeachment, the president struggled on for a time before he finally gave up. He was succeeded by his vice-president, Gerald Ford, who later pardoned Nixon, effectively closing the disastrous Watergate affair.

• **SEE ALSO**
Pages 8–9: 21 February 1972
President Nixon Visits China

• **FURTHER INFORMATION**
Books:
Watergate Scandal
by Heather Lehr Wagner
(Chelsea House Publishers, 2012)
Websites:
www.washingtonpost.com/watergate
Information from the *Washington Post* newspaper, which was prominent in investigating the cover-up.

Ethiopia's Emperor is Deposed

On 11 September, soldiers and police arrested members of the imperial family in various parts of Ethiopia. By the next morning, military units had strengthened their hold on the capital, Addis Ababa. Tanks and jeeps surrounded the emperor's Jubilee Palace. A group of officers, armed with sub-machine guns, entered the building and confronted their 82-year-old sovereign, Haile Selassie. The leader of the group, Major Debela Dinsa, accused the emperor of abusing his power and declared that his reign was over. Then Haile Selassie was escorted to a car – not one of his own limousines but, humiliatingly, a small Volkswagen Beetle. The fallen emperor was driven away and held at a military barracks.

The emperor's career

This ended Haile Selassie's remarkable career. As emperor of Ethiopia from 1930, he had tried to modernize his large, ancient but poor country. Then, in 1935, Italy's fascist dictator Benito Mussolini decided to conquer Ethiopia and turn it into a colony. The Ethiopians conducted a brave but hopeless struggle against the invaders, and in 1936 Haile Selassie was forced into exile. He was restored to the throne in 1941, during World War II.

Haile Selassie and his bodyguards during the most heroic period of the emperor's career, the 1935 invasion of Ethiopia by Italy.

What the papers said

The dismal latter part of Haile Selassie's internal policies should not obscure his earlier career. He led resistance to the Italian invasion of 1935. He unified the country, and initiated early reforms. But he stayed too long. The ex-Emperor['s] ... attitude ... made it impossible for him to understand why education and hand outs of land, food, and money were regarded not just as gifts ... but as rights. He never understood why these whetted rather than satisfied appetites ... he became increasingly out of touch ... and for service to his people substituted corruption and ... expensive political patronage.

The Guardian, 13 September 1974

The Ethiopian emperor Haile Selassie in old age, a few months before he was overthrown. Under his rule, Ethiopia remained a desperately poor country. However, those who took power after him were no more successful.

His dignified resistance to the Italians made him a hero to many Africans. When the colonial era ended, he became one of the founders of the Organization of African Unity, with its headquarters at Addis Ababa.

Failure and fall

However, Haile Selassie failed to solve Ethiopia's problems. The country remained poor even by African standards. A minority of landowning families held all real power, and little progress was made towards democracy. In 1960 Ethiopia took over neighbouring Eritrea, and fierce Eritrean resistance locked the Ethiopian army into a long and costly struggle. When drought and famine struck central Ethiopia, the emperor's government mishandled the situation. Corrupt officials stole resources intended for starving people, and many thousands died.

By February 1974 the country was suffering from inflation and unemployment. The armed forces began to take over. Haile Selassie became increasingly isolated and powerless, and few were surprised when he was deposed. In August 1975 his death was announced; he may have been murdered by his captors. Ethiopia was ruled by a military committee, the Dergue, and then by the ruthless Major Mengistu Haile Mariam. Years of tyranny, fruitless wars and chaos followed until Mengistu's regime collapsed in 1991.

- **SEE ALSO**
  Pages 26–27: 20 November 1975
  General Franco Dies

- **FURTHER INFORMATION**
  📖 Books:
  It's Cool to Learn About Countries: Ethiopia
  by Barbara A Somervill
  (Cherry Lake Publishing, 2011)
  Websites:
  www.time.com/time/magazine/article/
  0,9171,908740,00.html
  'The End of the Lion of Judah'

Saigon Falls to the North Vietnamese

By 29 April, the war was as good as over. The South Vietnamese army had collapsed and the forces of communist North Vietnam were poised to take Saigon, the capital of the South. Many people had fled from the city, and abandoned foreign embassies were being looted. However, the US embassy was still occupied. It was a fortress protected by high walls, barbed wire and a contingent of US Marines.

Dramatic events were unfolding there. The embassy compound was crowded with Americans and Vietnamese, desperate to leave the country. Many more Vietnamese were outside, frantically trying to climb in. One after another, US helicopters landed in the compound and, dangerously overcrowded, carried their passengers to aircraft carriers waiting off the coast. Hours later, North Vietnamese tanks reached the centre of Saigon and the South's president surrendered unconditionally.

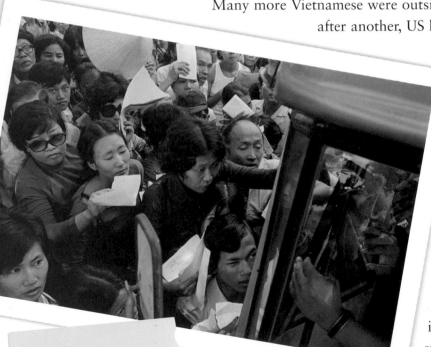

As the Vietnam War comes to an end, South Vietnamese queue, waving identity documents, to board a bus that will take them to the US Embassy and, they hope, safety.

The long struggle

The communist victory ended a conflict that went back to a time when Vietnam was a French colony. By the 1950s the country was divided into independent northern and southern states. A new struggle began in which South Vietnam came under attack from guerrilla fighters inside the country, unofficially backed by North Vietnam. The US intervened to support South Vietnam and found itself pouring in more and more troops and materials. As the 1960s went on, American casualties mounted. Despite its huge firepower and devastating bombing raids on the North, the US seemed unable to win. Many Americans began to oppose the war, and the country became bitterly divided. Finally, the United States and North

Vietnam made peace, and by 1973 the US had withdrawn all its forces. The war between North and South went on, however, and it became clear that US efforts to strengthen the South Vietnamese army had failed. The victorious North Vietnamese surged forward to take Saigon.

Pol Pot's atrocities

In the same year, 1975, communist forces took control of two neighbouring ex-French colonies, Cambodia and Laos. For them, and for Vietnam, rebuilding a devastated country was an immense task. But in Cambodia worse was to come. Led by Pol Pot, the communist Khmer Rouge introduced brutal and radical policies that uprooted huge numbers of people. At least a million Cambodians were killed by the regime or starved in the chaotic conditions it created. Their ordeal only ended in 1979 when the Vietnamese invaded the country and set up a less extreme government.

A pile of skulls, part of the Choeng Ek Memorial in Cambodia. It was set up to remember the countless victims of the Khmer Rouge regime, which ruled the country 1975–79.

⊙ eye witness

As the first Chinook helicopter made its precarious landing, its rotors slashed into a tree, and the snapping branches sounded like gunfire.... The helicopter's capacity was fifty [people], but it lifted off with seventy. The pilot's skill was breathtaking.... At six-fifteen p.m. it was my turn.... The helicopter tilted, rose, dropped sharply, then climbed as if laden with rocks.... There was small-arms fire around us, but they were letting us go; and when the South China Sea lay beneath us, the pilot, who was red-eyed with fatigue ... lit up a cigarette and handed the packet around.

John Pilger, *The Last Day* (Mirror Group Books, 1975)

- **SEE ALSO**
  Pages 6–7: 16 December 1971
  Bangladesh is Born
  Pages 36–37: 1 February 1979
  Ayatollah Khomeini Returns to Iran

- **FURTHER INFORMATION**
  📖 Books:
  The Fall of Saigon by Mary Englar (Compass Point Books, 2008)
  Websites:
  http://news.bbc.co.uk/1/shared/spl/hi/asia_pac /05/vietnam_war/html/fall_of_saigon.stm
  The fall of Saigon

General Franco Dies

Following several heart attacks and severe peritonitis, Spain's 83-year-old dictator, Francisco Franco, died on 20 November. As Franco had intended, Prince Juan Carlos became king of Spain and the new head of state. Franco had supervised Juan Carlos's education and hoped that the king would uphold the political system. However, Franco's followers suspected – rightly – that Juan Carlos wanted a democratic monarchy. Many of them held powerful positions, so the political situation was tense and complicated.

The dictatorship

Franco had established his dictatorship in 1939 at the end of a ferocious civil war. His regime combined traditional conservative and Catholic values with elements of Fascism inspired by Franco's one-time allies, Fascist Italy and Nazi Germany. During his 36-year rule, the liberals, socialists and communists who had opposed him in the Civil War were mercilessly hounded. In the 1970s Spain was still a country in which political parties, independent trade unions, strikes and free elections were forbidden.

The coffined body of Francisco Franco, the general who won the Spanish Civil War and was dictator of Spain from 1939 until his death in 1975.

Stealthy change

By this time, Franco's Spain was out of step with the rest of prosperous, democratic Western Europe. In 1974, a revolution in neighbouring Portugal overthrew the only other dictatorship in the region. But even after Franco's death it was hard to bring about change in Spain because of the carefully constructed system he had left behind him. Juan Carlos moved cautiously, working within the existing laws. A direct move towards democracy, however popular, risked a coup by military leaders loyal to their old chief. Without denouncing Franco, Juan Carlos manoeuvred for months to replace followers of the dictator who held key positions. The decisive moment came in July 1976, when the king was able to name a liberal-minded official, Adolfo Suárez, as his prime minister. Political parties were legalized and free elections were held. By the end of 1978, the Francoist state was being dismantled and a new, democratic constitution had been drawn up and approved.

The failed coup

The early years of democratic Spain were troubled, and in February 1981 the long-feared coup attempt occurred. Civil Guards (military-style police) seized the parliament building and held its members as hostages. But the king and millions of demonstrators condemned the coup, which rapidly collapsed. The episode showed that democracy had taken a firm hold in Spain. This was confirmed in 1982 when the Socialist Party won the elections and was able to take office peacefully.

King Juan Carlos I of Spain signs the country's 1978 constitution. It ended the political system set up by Franco and made Spain a fully democratic state.

What the papers said

While the official condolences were going on, first reports said that the announcement of the dictator's death brought an explosion of joy.... In one street in a fashionable part of Madrid while mass for Franco was being held in the church, less than 100 yards away a popular bar was packed with smiling and laughing people drinking to the dawn of a new era free from fascism.... Abroad, despite the spate of official condolences, there was hardly a personal tribute among them, and there was a chorus of hope for future democracy in Spain.

Sam Russell, *Morning Star*, 21 November 1975

- **SEE ALSO**
  Pages 22–23: 12 September 1974
  Ethiopia's Emperor is Deposed

- **FURTHER INFORMATION**
  📖 Books:
  Spain by Barbara A Somervill
  (Children's Press, 2012)
  🖱 Websites:
  http://news.bbc.co.uk/1/hi/world/europe/country
  _profiles/992004.stm
  Spain timeline and information about Franco

Concorde Goes into Service

Aircraft capable of supersonic flight – faster than the speed of sound – had been manufactured since 1947. But such aircraft had always been built for military purposes. Concorde was something new and thrilling – an airliner that could hold a hundred passengers and travel across oceans and continents while cruising at 2,150 kilometres an hour, twice the speed of sound. Concorde was a joint venture, developed and funded by the British and French governments. So the first passenger flights were arranged to begin simultaneously in the two countries.

On 21 January 1976, British Airways' Concorde 206 left Heathrow Airport for Bahrain in the Persian Gulf. Air France flew from Orly Airport, via Dakar in Senegal, to Rio de Janeiro in Brazil. Flights to the United States were not immediately possible because of objections to the sonic boom, the explosive sound heard when the aircraft broke the sound barrier. The objections were overcome, and from November 1977 the daily flights from Paris and London to New York became the most important

British Airways' Concorde 206 lifts off from Heathrow Airport on its first passenger flight to Bahrain. At the same time an Air France Concorde took off from Paris for Rio de Janeiro.

The end of the Concorde story, November 2003. With Concorde about to retire, one of the British Airways' fleet is towed towards lower Manhattan, where it will be given an honoured place in New York's Intrepid Sea, Air and Space Museum.

part of Concorde's schedule. The transatlantic crossing usually took about three and a half hours, at least twice as fast as conventional, 'sub-sonic' aircraft. Because the world is divided into different time zones, when Concordes travelled westward, they arrived at a clock time earlier than the one at which they had left!

The striking, bird-like image of Concorde's distinctive 'droop' nose and double-delta-shaped wings became known all over the world. These were functional as well as attractive features, typical of the aircraft's advanced technology. Worked on all through the 1960s and test-flown from 1969, Concorde was an expensive project. The original intention was to sell the aircraft to the airlines of other countries, but events such as the 1973 oil crisis put off potential customers. In the long run, Britain and France probably benefited from their exclusive right to Concorde's prestige. During their lifetime, Concordes set up a number of world speed records. There was a single serious accident in 2000, when a crash at Gonesse in France killed 113 people. This was a factor in the decision to retire Concorde. Its farewell flight, on 26 November 2003, marked the end of an impressive and glamorous career.

eye witness

On 21 January 1976 I stood with my wife, camera at the ready, at the take-off end of runway 28L.… Around us were crowds of people, some wearing … 'service' earphones connected to electronic devices wired up to microphones on poles. Concorde would not start … unrecorded! We listened to a local radio broadcast. At 11.40 precisely the commentator announced that Concorde had begun to roll. Next came the distinctive sound of the four reheated Olympus engines. Then Concorde GBOAA came in view, climbing out over the approach lights of the reciprocal runway, with the undercarriage retracting. Commercial supersonic services had begun.

Christopher Orlebar, *The Concorde Story* (Osprey, 2004)

- **SEE ALSO**
Pages 30–31: 20 July 1976
Viking 1 Lands on Mars

- **FURTHER INFORMATION**
  Books:
  The Complete History of Aviation: From Ballooning to Supersonic Flight by Robert Curley (Rosen Education Service, 2011)
  Websites:
  www.britishairways.com/concorde
  British Airways' Celebrating Concorde website

Viking 1 Lands on Mars

Viking 1 and Viking 2 were American space probes – unmanned craft despatched by NASA, the organization that ran the US space programme. Each probe consisted of an orbiter, designed to keep flying steadily round the planet, and a lander that would descend to the surface. Both orbiters and landers were able to send images and data back to earth. If the landers remained operational after reaching the surface of Mars, they would provide the first close-up views of a planet that had always had a romantic and mysterious reputation.

The first images

On 20 July, Viking 1's lander arrived intact on the surface. Within days, the images it sent back to earth had been processed and published. It also sent back analyses of soil samples and other data. The lander had set down on an irregular, cratered area, and so Viking 2's descent was rescheduled so that it could land on more suitable terrain. It came down on the other side of the planet in September 1976. The Viking images showed a dry, dusty, rock-strewn surface, and the data they sent back gave no support to the often expressed idea that Mars was, or had once been, capable of sustaining life. However, decades later in 2012, the Mars rover robot found clear evidence that there had once been water on Mars.

An image of the dry, rocky surface of the planet Mars, sent back to earth by the US probe Viking Lander 2. Part of the lander can be seen at the front of the picture.

Further into space

In 1969 the United States scored an immense triumph by putting its astronauts on the moon. Other moon flights followed until 1972, but further exploration of the solar system could only be carried out by unmanned craft. The rival superpowers, the United States and the Soviet Union, continued to dominate space exploration. In 1974, NASA's Mariner 10 flew past Mercury, the planet nearest the sun. The following year, the Soviet probe Venera 9 landed on the surface of Venus, long hidden from astronomers beneath dense clouds, and sent back the first images. The United States then sent probes on much longer journeys, towards the outer planets of the solar system.

Space stations and satellites

Meanwhile, astronauts found a new role in the space stations that had begun orbiting the earth. Salyut 1, launched in 1971, was the first of a series of Soviet stations, followed in 1973 by the USA's Skylab. Space stations were used primarily for scientific research, but by the end of the 1970s many other artificial satellites were orbiting the earth, used for many purposes, including telephone and TV communications and military spying.

A dramatic view of the Skylab space station, taken from space by the associated Skylab 4 mission. Skylab was the USA's first space station, visited by human crews and orbiting the earth from 1973 to 1979.

⊙ eye witness

Mike Carr recalled his feelings when the ... team members began to look at the ... data in detail. 'We were just astounded – both a mixture of elation and shock.' They were elated at the quality and detail of the pictures but shocked at what they saw. All their data-processing schedules had been based on a preconceived notion of what Mars should look like, and this was not it.... All that they saw – the etched surfaces, the multitude of craters and islands in the channels ... told them that the ... site was not a suitable place to land.

E C and L N Ezell, *On Mars: Exploration of the Red Planet 1958–1978* (NASA History Series, 1984)

- **SEE ALSO**
  Pages 28–29: 21 January 1976
  Concorde Goes into Service

- **FURTHER INFORMATION**
  📖 Books:
  Far-Out Guide to Mars
  by Mary Kay Carson (Bailey Books, 2010)
  🖱 Websites:
  http://mars.jpl.nasa.gov/participate/funzone
  NASA site about Mars exploration for kids

The Sex Pistols on Top of the Pops

On 14 July 1977, a video of the Sex Pistols was shown on Britain's leading pop TV programme, *Top of the Pops*. The group had now definitely become mainstream national performers. Their rise to fame had begun only two years earlier when they played their first gig as the Sex Pistols with Johnny Rotten as lead singer. Their harsh, driving punk rock style matched the angrily rebellious mood of songs like 'Anarchy in the UK' and 'God Save the Queen', which described Queen Elizabeth II as reigning over a 'fascist regime'. In December 1976 the group had become notorious through a TV programme in which one of them, encouraged by the interviewer, had sworn copiously. Many people were outraged by the Sex Pistols and they were banned at some venues. But they made headlines. Despite protests, *Top of the Pops* showed them performing their latest hit, 'Pretty Vacant', dedicated to British youth.

International punk

Punk was a lifestyle as well as a type of music. Its young fans – punks – had their own distinctive look, with short, spiky hair and torn, safety-pin-decorated clothes. Both the music and the style first took shape in New York. Rock music had always had a wild, rebellious image, but by the early 1970s 'glam rock' and 'prog rock' had developed in a more showy, elaborate, technique-conscious direction.

However, some bands had continued to play in harder, more direct styles, inspiring punk performers such as Patti Smith and the Ramones who began to make their mark in 1974. Punk spread across the United States and became an international trend, not only in Britain

What the papers said

Various singers caressed the hand-mike with drooling narcissism [self-love], as though it were a stick of lip salve. The comically horrendous Sex Pistols on Thursday's *Top of the Pops* (BBC1) turned the same device into a Black and Decker power drill. They 'sang' like a group that wanted to punch holes in your knee-caps. The day cannot be too long delayed when showbiz will start doling out Death Achievement Awards, a prize to be won after making as many people as possible as sick as possible in no less time than it takes to pierce an ear-lobe with a safety-pin.

Dennis Potter, *The Sunday Times*, 17 July 1977

The British band the Sex Pistols, fronted by Johnny Rotten, performs in the USA. The band made a highly controversial impact.

(the Sex Pistols, the Clash,
the Damned) but in Australia (the Saints),
Canada (the Diodes) and Western Europe.

After punk

Having changed the direction of popular music, punk continued to
evolve. In January 1978 the Sex Pistols broke up, while new or
re-formed bands were appearing all the time. One trend was
represented by hardcore in the United States and Oi! and anarcho-
punk in Britain. It went even further in presenting aggressive
political messages, and the discordant sound and shouted lyrics
deliberately rejected traditional musical skills and melody.
By contrast, New Wave and Pop Punk moved closer to
popular and dance music, allowing bands such as
Blondie and Talking Heads to achieve mainstream
success. Revived from time to time, punk influenced
later anti-mainstream trends such as alternative rock
and indie (music on independent labels).

- **FURTHER INFORMATION**
- 📖 Books:
  Punk: Music, Fashion, Attitude!
  by Charlotte Guillain (Raintree, 2010)
- Websites:
  http://library.rockhall.com/content.php?
  pid=310399
  Rock 'n' roll hall of fame site

Karol Wojtyla is Elected Pope

The pope is the head of the worldwide Roman Catholic Church. He rules Vatican City, a tiny independent state in Rome, the capital of Italy. When a pope dies, the College of Cardinals (leading churchmen) meets in the Sistine Chapel in the Vatican to elect his successor. There are usually several ballots (voting sessions) before one of the candidates receives enough support to be declared the new pope.

A surprise choice

The election is a dramatic event. Black smoke rises from the chapel chimney after each unsuccessful ballot; when the smoke is white, the world knows that the choice has been made. A huge crowd waits eagerly for the result in Rome's St Peter's Square. The election in October 1978 was decided after eight ballots held over two days. White smoke rose from the chapel window at 6.18 p.m. on 16 October. The cardinals' choice was a surprise – 58-year-old Karol Wojtyla, archbishop of Krakow in Poland. He was the first-ever Polish pope and the first non-Italian for 455 years. When elected, a pope chooses the name he wishes to be known by. Wojtyla wished to pay tribute to his frail predecessor, John Paul I, whose reign lasted only 33 days. The new pope became John Paul II.

October 1978: a huge crowd in St Peter's Square, Rome, waits to learn who is to be the new pope. Karol Wojtyla was elected and took the name John Paul II.

Papal globe-trotter

One of his first actions broke with tradition. Instead of a few words in Latin, John Paul II, master of many languages, spoke eloquently in Italian to the delighted crowd in St Peter's Square. This popular touch proved to be typical. Previous popes had travelled very little, but John Paul II visited over a hundred countries all over the world. He was greeted by vast crowds and moved among them, standing up in a specially designed car, the 'popemobile'. He made an extraordinary personal impact on both Catholics and non-Catholics. This public exposure was not risk-free. There were several attempts to assassinate him, notably in 1981 when he was seriously wounded by a gunman.

John Paul II preached international peace and reconciliation between religions. Yet his reign had controversial aspects. For example, he strongly asserted traditional teachings on topics such as contraception, felt by some sections of the Church to need modernizing. John Paul II lived to see the end of communism in his native Poland and the rest of Eastern Europe. His long reign ended with his death in 2005.

A smiling Pope John Paul II is greeted by adoring crowds during his weekly general audience in St Peter's Church, Rome.

eye witness

I defended my opinion openly before the conclave. I said that 'It's time to change the system and to vote for a non-Italian'.... There was enormous tension the whole time.... When the number of votes for him [Wojtyla] approached one-half [of the votes needed to elect him] he cast away his pencil and sat up straight. He was red in the face. Then he was holding his head in his hands. My impression was that he was completely confused. Then the final majority number turned up. He had two-thirds of the vote plus one.

Cardinal Franz König, quoted in Tad Szulc, *Pope John Paul II* (Scribner, 1995)

- **FURTHER INFORMATION**
- Books:
  Pope John Paul II by Gary Smailes (Waverley Books, 2009)
- Websites:
  http://news.bbc.co.uk/1/hi/in_depth/world/pope_john_paul_ii/default.stm
  Pope John Paul II

Ayatollah Khomeini Returns to Iran

After 15 years of exile, the 78-year-old Ayatollah Khomeini flew into Tehran, the capital of Iran. As his title, ayatollah, indicated, he was a senior Muslim religious figure. But for Iranians he was above all a symbol of popular resistance to the shah (king) of Iran, who had been overthrown a fortnight earlier. The situation was still chaotic, and the stern, bearded Khomeini was hailed as a saviour. On his arrival, a million people greeted him rapturously, brandishing his picture.

Returned from exile, Ayatollah Khomeini is acclaimed at his home by his massed supporters.

Iran under the shah

Iran was one of several Middle Eastern countries in which modern and traditional lifestyles co-existed uneasily. It was an oil-rich country, making substantial, if uneven, economic progress. Until 1979, the shah seemed an impressive figure, internationally admired for modernizing his country. But in Iran his modernizing, and his close ties to the United States, outraged traditionalists like the Ayatollah Khomeini, who was exiled for opposing greater freedom for women and other reforms. At the same time, liberals and other pro-reform groups were angered by the lack of democracy in Iran. The shah held absolute power, and his secret police, SAVAK, were notorious for torturing and murdering the regime's opponents.

The revolution

The shah appeared to be in complete control until January 1979, when an official newspaper published an attack on the exiled Khomeini. Some demonstrators protested, troops fired on them, and street demonstrations spread all over the country. The shah mishandled the situation. He used enough force to anger people, but not enough to cow them, and the concessions he made came too late. The situation spiralled out of control, and the shah fled the country on 16 January 1979.

The Islamic Republic

Soon after Khomeini's return, Iran was proclaimed an Islamic Republic. The Muslim religion had become a major political force. Then the shah, who had cancer, was admitted to the United States. Most Iranians believed that the USA was plotting with the shah, and in November 1979 Iranian students took over the US embassy in Tehran and held its staff as hostages. Anti-American feeling swept Iran, the moderate government resigned, and liberal and other secular groups were swept aside. Iran became a state in which ayatollahs supervised the government, and society was dominated by conservative Islamic ideas and practices (Islamic fundamentalism). From the 1980s, the Iranian government was a revolutionary force in the Muslim world, implacably hostile to the United States and Western values.

Iranians stand on top of the US Embassy wall and burn an American flag. Seizing the embassy and taking hostages from its staff, students set off a crisis that lasted until 1981.

eye witness

Despite the prospect of serious days ahead, yesterday was one of celebration and jubilation for the followers of the man whom some see as a mystical Imam, or leader.... Throughout the city, people climbed trees or perched on the tops of bus shelters, telephone boxes, garden walls or railings to get a glimpse of Khomeini. His portrait was everywhere, on walls and windows, strung across streets and on pennants waved by the crowds. It was a welcome reminiscent of ... Hollywood films depicting the return of a Roman Emperor ... but instead of a cast of thousands it had a cast of millions.

James Allen, *Daily Telegraph*, 2 February 1979

- **SEE ALSO**
  Pages 6–7: 16 December 1971
  Bangladesh is Born
  Pages 24–25: 29 April 1975
  Saigon Falls to the North Vietnamese

- **FURTHER INFORMATION**
  Books:
  The Iranian Revolution
  by Heather Lehr Wagner
  (Chelsea House Publishers, 2010)
  Websites:
  http://kids.nationalgeographic.com/kids/places
  /find/iran
  National Geographic site about Iran

Soviet Forces Enter Afghanistan

Afghan president Hafizullah Amin holds a press conference. Having seized power, he was soon to be overthrown in his turn.

It began when thousands of airborne Soviet troops were landed at the airport outside Kabul, the capital of Afghanistan. The communist Afghan government was facing a major rebellion and had been asking its Soviet allies to send troops and military supplies since early 1979. But the Soviets had plans of their own. On 27 December, Soviet units occupied key points in Kabul and stormed the presidential palace. The president, Hafizullah Amin, was killed and another communist, Babrak Karmal, was installed as the new leader. Karmal, too, needed Soviet help, and ground troops poured into the country from the north.

Communist Afghanistan

Afghanistan was a poor, economically backward Muslim country in which local and tribal loyalties were strong. Communism seemed unlikely to win wide support in such a society, despite the influence of Afghanistan's mighty neighbour, the Soviet Union. However, in April 1978 the Afghan army overthrew the existing regime and the communist PDPA (People's Democratic Party of Afghanistan) took over the government. Its policies sparked a series of rebellions which were soon being funded and supplied by the United States. At first the Soviet leaders were reluctant to intervene and sent only limited military assistance. However, they came to believe that Amin's brutal methods were making the situation worse, and that the United States might move in, possibly after doing

⊙ eye witness

I returned again [to Afghanistan] as a journalist in the autumn of 1979.... Outwardly, the Afghan capital appeared quite normal.... Nevertheless, the tension, the insecurity, the growing hatred for the communists were apparent just beneath the surface.... With the growth of repression ... and the fighting constantly spreading to new fronts in the countryside, it was evident that something would have to break sooner or later; another coup perhaps, an army uprising, or even a rebel takeover of Kabul. Few people expected anything as drastic as the Soviet intervention.

Edward R Girardit, *Afghanistan: The Soviet War* (Croom Helm, 1985)

A group of Afghan fighters, part of the resistance to the communist regime and the Soviet army. With US help they rapidly became much better armed.

a deal with Amin himself. Consequently the Soviets replaced Amin with Karmal, the leader of a rival faction in the PDPA. Within a few months there were 80,000 Soviet troops in Afghanistan, and the rebel groups that tried to resist them in open warfare were crushed with ruthless efficiency.

A Soviet blunder

Nevertheless, the Soviet intervention in Afghanistan was a serious mistake. The United States and its allies denounced it as an invasion, and most of the Muslim world was angered. During the 1970s, relations between the superpowers had improved, but the Afghanistan issue led to renewed hostility, which persisted into the 1980s. The Soviets' early military successes failed to end Afghan resistance, and groups of guerrillas, known as mujahideen (warriors), began to use hit-and-run tactics against Soviet and government forces. This proved highly effective in Afghanistan's mountainous terrain. For the Soviets, Afghanistan soon turned into a nightmare, often compared with the demoralizing US involvement in Vietnam. Afghanistan itself would become a flashpoint in world politics for decades to come.

• **FURTHER INFORMATION**
📖 Books:
The War in Afghanistan
by Brian Williams (Franklin Watts, 2010)
🖰 Websites:
www.globalresearch.ca/articles/BRZ110A.html
A revealing interview with a US presidential adviser

Britain Joins the Common Market

Britain's prime minister, Edward Heath, flew into the Belgian capital, Brussels, on 22 January. He was joined by two of his ministers and members of other British political parties. They were driven to the Palais d'Egmont (Egmont Palace), where European leaders were waiting. As Heath walked up the marble staircase, a young woman flung a pot of ink at his head. She was a complete stranger to the prime minister, with a grievance that had nothing to do with his business in Brussels. There was a delay while Heath was cleaned up and put on a fresh suit and shirt. Then he went into the hall and signed the Treaty of Accession to the European Communities (EC), which most British people called the Common Market.

The growth of the Common Market

The Common Market developed from the European Coal and Steel Community, set up in 1951 by West Germany, France, Italy, Belgium, the Netherlands and Luxembourg. The object of the community was to do away with barriers to trading and transporting coal and iron within the territories of 'the Six'. Economically advantageous, this arrangement was also intended to bind together six nations that had often in the past been involved in wars. The experiment was so successful that the 1957 Treaty of Rome widened the scope of the original organization. It became the European Economic Community (EEC), committed to achieving the free movement of all goods, services and workers throughout its territories. The community was now run by its own commissioners and had its own parliament and court of justice.

Brussels, January 1972: Prime Minister Edward Heath signs the treaty committing Britain to join the Common Market.

Britain and the Common Market

At first, Britain made no attempt to join. But the community's success, and Britain's economic difficulties, persuaded political leaders to think again. In the 1960s, British attempts to enter the community were blocked by the president of France, Charles de Gaulle. After de Gaulle's death, Heath patiently negotiated an agreement. Many people and politicians were still against entering the Common Market, but after a tough parliamentary struggle the treaty was passed into British law in October 1972. On 1 January 1973 Britain became a full member of the EEC, along with Ireland and Denmark. The British decision was confirmed by a referendum in 1975. In 1993 the EEC became the European Union, and despite phases of unpopularity, it continued to expand over the next two decades.

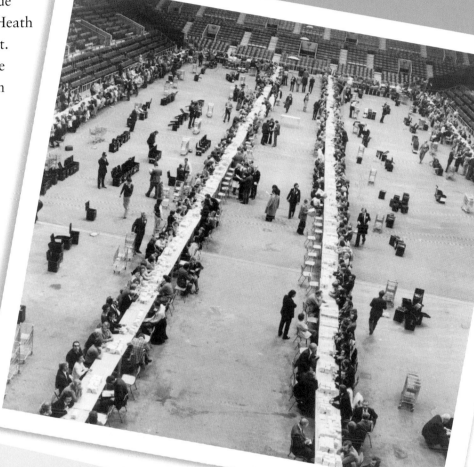

Counting the votes after the referendum in Britain on the Common Market: the majority voted for continued membership.

What the papers said

This transformation of ... Europe ... is a most colossal gamble. You can't really let Britain, Denmark, Ireland ... into the Common Market just by stretching the Rome Treaty ... some things have got to give.... To move to a common currency, a common defence policy and a real unity of purpose may take a generation ... or a lifetime ... or it may never happen.... All we know is that we've made a peaceful start. And that, with patience and persistence, we hope to build a strong and peaceful future for this our Continent of Europe.

Daily Mail, 24 January 1972

- **FURTHER INFORMATION**
- 📖 Books:
  The European Union
  by Peggy Kahn (Chelsea House Publishers, 2008)
- 🖰 Websites:
  europa.eu/abc/history/index_en.htm
  A chronological history of the EU with videos

30 JANUARY 1972

'Bloody Sunday'

In the morning, British troops appeared in force on the streets of Londonderry, Northern Ireland's second largest city. Northern Ireland was a province of the United Kingdom, bitterly divided between its Protestant and Catholic communities. In 1969 the British Army had been sent into the province and had been welcomed as protectors by the Catholics, the minority community. But relations had worsened, and the Catholics now saw the army as allies of the oppressive Protestant majority.

In Londonderry and the capital, Belfast, there were frequent riots in which Catholic youths stoned the troops, who responded by firing hard rubber bullets and water cannon. The gunmen of the IRA (Irish Republican Army) were a more serious threat than the youths, since they were prepared to kill soldiers in their fight against British rule.

A British soldier manhandles a civilian on 'Bloody Sunday', when troops shot dead 13 people during a civil rights march in Londonderry, Northern Ireland. Arguments about the events continue.

Firing on marchers

On 30 January the soldiers were manning barricades around the Catholic area of Londonderry. An afternoon march had been arranged by the Civil Rights Association, which campaigned for equal rights for Northern Irish Catholics. Though there might be bad behaviour on the march, it seemed strange to bring in so many troops, mostly equipped with rifles and sub-machine guns. The march started about 2.45 p.m. An hour later, there was rioting away from the main route, which the soldiers dealt with forcefully but without using live ammunition. Then, just before four o'clock, the shooting started on the main route. Paratroops opened fire and severely injured two men. A few minutes later, there were further shootings nearby, in a more crowded area. By late in the afternoon, 13 civilians had been killed and 14 wounded. Several of the dead had been shot in the back. Some soldiers claimed they had sighted civilians carrying bombs or guns, but this was never proved. No weapons were found anywhere near the scene.

Inconclusive inquiries

The first official inquiry put most of the blame on the marchers. But in 1974 the British government admitted that all the shot civilians were innocent victims, and paid compensation to their families. Many questions remained to be answered. A new inquiry (1998-2010) eventually reported that the victims were innocent and that the army was responsible for the killings. After 'Bloody Sunday', support for the IRA swelled, and violence raged in the province, spilling over into mainland Britain, until the late 1990s.

2 February 1972: the funeral procession of the 13 civilians killed on 'Bloody Sunday' leaves St Mary's Chapel.

 eye witness

What I saw next after that I couldn't believe…. An army troop carrier appeared, and it started coming slowly towards us down the street. A man was running away from it and they were chasing him…. He escaped somehow…. So then the troop carrier stopped, and out of it, or from out of another one that'd come along by its side, half a dozen soldiers jumped. They stood by the vehicle a minute: and then slowly and deliberately each one of them went down on one knee and started to fire deliberately into the crowd.

Sean Collins (9 years old in 1972), from an interview by Tony Parker, *New Statesman and Society*, January 1992

- **FURTHER INFORMATION**
- Books:
  The Troubles in Northern Ireland by Ivan Minnis (Heinemann, 2001)
- Websites:
  news.bbc.co.uk/hi/english/static/in_depth/ northern_ireland/2000/bloody_sunday/ map/default.stm
  An hour-by-hour account with street maps

Britain's First Woman Prime Minister

The early results of Britain's general election showed the Conservative Party in the lead. By the early afternoon it was clear that the Labour Government, led by James Callaghan, would have to resign. At 2.45 p.m. the Conservative leader, Margaret Thatcher, was summoned to Buckingham Palace, and in traditional fashion Queen Elizabeth II asked Thatcher to form a government. Then Thatcher met Ken Stowe, the top civil servant, who would be her principal private secretary. They drove from the palace, this time in the car reserved for the prime minister. It took them to 10 Downing Street, the prime minister's official residence. Outside the house, Margaret Thatcher made a speech promising to bring harmony and order to a nation that she believed was confused and divided.

The newly elected British prime minister Margaret Thatcher and her husband Denis wave to crowds outside her official London residence, 10 Downing Street.

A victory for women?

Thatcher was the first woman to lead a British political party, and she now became the first woman prime minister. The overwhelming majority of ministers and MPs were still men, so the event could be seen as a victory for sexual equality. The 1970s was the decade of 'Women's Lib' (Liberation), in which women pressed for equal pay, rights and respect. Without their marches and demonstrations, a woman might have found it impossible to become prime minister in 1979. However, Thatcher herself stood for rather different values and policies. She strongly disapproved of the way society and the economy had been organized since the 1940s. She wanted to 'roll back the state' – to end state control or regulation of industries, business and financial dealings. These, she claimed, held back individual initiative and slowed down Britain's economic progress.

Promise of change

Though Britain was a prosperous country, it was no longer a world leader, and many people feared that it was declining. Mrs Thatcher's message appealed to them, and so did her aim of limiting the power of the trade unions. Not long before the election, events played into her hands. During 1978–79, a series of strikes broke out. Some were brief but intensely annoying to ordinary people, notably the strike that left rubbish uncollected for five weeks. This 'winter of discontent' was believed to have played a great part in Thatcher's victory in May. Her government made a slow start, but in the 1980s, repeated election victories gave 'Thatcherism' the chance to change British society in a dramatic fashion.

Rubbish in a London street: an extreme example of the results of strikes that made the Labour government unpopular in 1978–79.

What the papers said

The people have decided. Their message … seems clear enough: this is, roughly translated: let's try some other way and hope it works better…. That Mrs Thatcher has created any sense of hope, albeit one tinged with anxiety, is her first success…. She takes office at a troubled time … a deepening world recession, with a nation inured to the thought of chronic decline, apparently unable to summon the will or the nerve, or the communal sense of purpose, to stop it. Can she succeed where so many have failed for so long?

The Observer, 6 May 1979

- **FURTHER INFORMATION**
  - Books:
    Madam Prime Minister: A Biography of Margaret Thatcher
    by Libby Hughes (iUniverse, 2000)
  - Websites:
    www.bbc.co.uk/history/people/margaret_thatcher
    Margaret Thatcher's career

People of the Decade

Muhammad Ali
(born 1942)
American boxer Muhammad Ali was the only heavyweight to win the world championship three times. Originally known as Cassius Clay, he took the name Muhammad Ali on converting to the Nation of Islam (Black Muslims). He was world champion 1964–1971, 1974–1978 and 1978–1979. For a heavyweight, Ali was unusually skilful and fast on his feet, as well as strong. An entertaining personality, he boasted amusingly in rhyme, but his most celebrated statement was 'I am the greatest!'

Idi Amin
(1924–2003)
A former British army officer, Idi Amin became chief of the Ugandan armed forces (1966–1970). In January 1971 he overthrew the government and made himself president. Apparently clownish, Amin proved to be a bloodthirsty tyrant. Ugandans of Asian descent were thrown out of the country, and many thousands of people from tribes that Amin disliked were tortured and killed. In 1979, following a successful invasion by Tanzanian forces and Ugandan rebels, Amin fled the country, dying in exile.

David Bowie
(born 1947)
The British rock singer, song writer and actor was at the height of his celebrity in the 1970s. His breakthrough second album was *Hunky Dory* (1971). Bowie mixed and varied musical styles, from glam rock to heavy metal. Bizarre titles (*The Rise and Fall of Ziggy Stardust and the Spiders from Mars*) were matched by Bowie's deliberately extreme self-presentation, for example heavily made up. Bowie's best-known film performance was as an alien in *The Man Who Fell to Earth* (1976).

Leonid Illych Brezhnev
(1906–1982)
Brezhnev was the leader of the Soviet Union from 1964, when he ousted Nikita Khrushchev. All through the 1970s the Soviet Union seemed formidable, but Brezhnev's attempts to match the United States in armaments and international influence were in fact seriously weakening it. Brezhnev and other ageing Soviet leaders failed to reform the stagnating economy, and the 1979 Soviet intervention in Afghanistan proved to be another serious mistake, contributing towards the eventual collapse of the Soviet Union in 1991.

Jimmy Carter
(born 1924)
US politician Jimmy Carter, a Democrat, became president in 1977. Carter played a leading role in making peace between Egypt and Israel. He strongly opposed Soviet intervention in Afghanistan, but his popularity slumped when he failed to rescue American embassy officials taken as hostages by Iranians. He was heavily defeated in the 1980 election by Ronald Reagan. However, Carter remained active on the international scene, helping to find peaceful solutions to several crises.

Nadia Comaneci
(born 1961)
In training from the age of six, the Romanian gymnast Nadia Comaneci was a world-class competitor by the mid-1970s. At the 1976 Olympics in Montreal, Canada, her tiny, slender, 14-year-old figure and phenomenal performance made her a star. She became the first gymnast to achieve a perfect score of 10, and went on to achieve seven such scores. She shone again at the 1980 Moscow Olympics before retiring in 1984.

Yves Saint Laurent
(1936–2008)
Algerian-born fashion designer who settled in Paris, where he worked for the famous Christian Dior fashion house, becoming its head in 1957. In 1962 he founded his own fashion house, later opening a chain of boutiques (small dress shops) selling ready-to-wear clothes. Saint Laurent's designs were highly influential, notably the trouser suits so popular with the new breed of 1970s businesswomen. Perfumes, colognes, men's clothing and other products also carried the Saint Laurent label.

Anwar Sadat
(1918–1981)
As president of Egypt (1970–1981), Sadat radically changed his country's policies. He ended Egypt's close relations with the Soviet Union and sought the friendship of the United States. He launched the 1973 Yom Kippur War against Israel, but later worked to secure a peace treaty. After it was signed in March 1979, Egypt recovered the Israeli-occupied Sinai peninsula. Many Arabs were angered by the treaty, and Egypt's severe economic problems also made Sadat unpopular, leading to his assassination in 1981.

Mother Teresa
(1910–1997)
A Roman Catholic nun, Mother Teresa became famous for her work in India, where her hostel in Calcutta (now Kolkata) cared for the old, the sick and the dying. In 1950 she founded the Order of the Missionaries of Charity, which established hostels in many parts of the world. Much honoured in the 1970s, Mother Teresa was awarded the Nobel Prize for Peace in 1979. In 2003 she was beatified (declared blessed) by Pope John Paul II.

Glossary

acumen Shrewdness or intelligence.

autonomy Self-government. A region or country is described as autonomous when it runs its own affairs but is not completely independent. For example, it may be responsible to a central government which keeps control of certain big decisions such as making war or peace.

ballot A vote, or the process of voting.

bazooka A tube-shaped infantry weapon that fires armour-piercing missiles.

CIA The Central Intelligence Agency, the organization that conducts spying, secret information-gathering and similar missions for the US government.

colonial era The period when European states possessed empires, governing peoples on other continents. The British Empire was the largest of the colonial empires.

commando A member of the armed forces who has been trained in special operations skills, for example night raiding on enemy positions.

communism A political system in which the state owns most property and controls economic activity. In practice, the Soviet Union and other communist states were run exclusively by their Communist Parties.

conclave A secret or private meeting, especially the conclave of cardinals held to elect a new pope.

conservative Opposed to change or believing that changes should be introduced only slowly and cautiously.

contraception The prevention of pregnancy by artificial means.

coup A sudden seizure of power.

Cultural Revolution The campaign launched in 1966 by the Chinese communist leader Mao Zedong. It was intended to revive China's revolutionary spirit but in fact proved oppressive and created chaotic conditions.

democracy A political system in which the citizens elect, and can change, their leaders.

Democrat A member or supporter of the Democrats, one of the USA's two main political parties.

détente A relaxation of the tensions between states with conflicting aims or ideas.

dictatorship A political system or situation in which a country is ruled by one person or a small group, without the consent of its people.

embargo A government order that forbids citizens to trade with a country regarded as hostile.

fascist A person, party or government that favours a military-style dictatorship and values obedience rather than freedom.

guerrillas Fighters who wage hit-and-run warfare, usually against a stronger enemy. They often take advantage of a mountainous or jungle environment in which they can hide.

hijack To seize control illegally of a ship, plane or vehicle. The intention is usually to hold the passengers as hostages while making political demands, or to transport the hijackers to a particular destination.

inflation Rising prices.

IRA The Irish Republican Army. Until the late 1990s, the IRA was an armed group aiming to overthrow the Northern Irish state and unite the region with the Irish Republic.

liberal A word that has many meanings, but generally suggests tolerance, open-mindedness and willingness to change.

Khmer Rouge The communist movement in Cambodia.

martial law Military law, which is swifter, less fair and harsher than the ordinary laws under which citizens live. In emergencies, martial law is often declared, replacing the ordinary laws until normality returns.

motorcade A procession of cars, carrying one or more famous or powerful individuals.

nationalize To take a firm or industry into state ownership.

radical A person or policy favouring fundamental and far-reaching change.

recession An economic downturn, often featuring high unemployment, falling production of goods and shrinking markets.

referendum A ballot in which all of a country's citizens vote to decide a single issue.

repartee Swift or clever responses made in conversation.

socialist A person who believes in socialism, a political system in which a country's main industries are owned and run by the state for the general benefit.

Soviet Union A huge state, also known as the USSR. Though often referred to as 'Russia', it actually consisted of present-day Russia and a number of other East European, Baltic and Central Asian countries. The leading communist power, the Soviet Union existed from 1922 to 1991.

Index

Page numbers in **bold** refer to illustrations